Index

About the Author

Elizabeth Raum has worked as a teacher, librarian, and writer. She has written dozens of books for young readers. She really enjoyed learning more about snakes. "Snakes are amazing," she says. "But I wouldn't want one for a pet." Visit her website at http://www. elizabethraum.net.

Read More

Jennings, Terry J. *Reptile Park*. Mankato, Minn:
QEB, 2010.

White, Nancy and Raoul Bain. *King Cobras:
the Biggest Venomous Snakes of All!* New York:
Bearport, 2009.

Willebrandt, Avery. *Spitting Cobra*. New York:
Gareth Stevens, 2012.

Websites

BBC Nature Wildlife
http://www.bbc.co.uk/nature/life/Naja

**National Geographic Kids Creature Feature:
King Cobra**
*http://animals.nationalgeographic.com/animals/reptiles/
king-cobra/*

San Diego Zoo's Animal Bytes: Cobra
http://www.sandiegozoo.org/animalbytes/t-cobra.html

Cobras

BY ELIZABETH RAUM

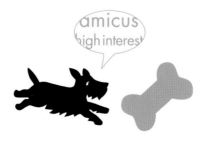

amicus
high interest

Amicus High Interest is an imprint of Amicus
P.O. Box 1329, Mankato, MN 56002
www.amicuspublishing.us

Library of Congress Cataloging-in-Publication Data
Raum, Elizabeth.
 Cobras / by Elizabeth Raum.
    pages cm. -- (Snakes)
 Includes index.
 Summary: "Explains cobras, especially the king cobra,
including what they eat, where they live, and information
about their life cycle and interaction with humans"--Provided
by publisher.
 Audience: K to Grade 3.
 ISBN 978-1-60753-373-3 (library binding) -- ISBN 978-1-
60753-421-1 (ebook)
 1. Cobras--Juvenile literature. I. Title.
 QL666.O64R38 2014
 597.96'42--dc23
                                    2012036389

Editor   Wendy Dieker
Series Designer   Kathleen Petelinsek
Page production   Red Line Editorial, Inc.

Photo Credits
iStockphoto, cover; Shutterstock Images, 4, 7; iStockphoto/
Thinkstock, 8, 28; Heiko Kiera/Shutterstock Images, 11;
Animals Animals/SuperStock, 12; Biosphoto/SuperStock,
15; Rhys Mansel/123RF, 16; Anton Rostovsky/iStockphoto,
18; Digital Vision/Thinkstock, 21; Angelo Giampiccolo/
Shutterstock Images, 22; Kobchai Matasurawit/123RF, 24;
Steven Cooper/123RF, 27

Printed in the United States at Corporate Graphics in North
Mankato, Minnesota
4-2013/1149
10 9 8 7 6 5 4 3 2 1

Table of Contents

A cobra opens its hood. Stay away from this snake!

 Q Why are elephants afraid?

Danger!

When the cobra lifts its head, watch out! The cobra flattens its neck. The neck ribs stretch to form a hood. The cobra is saying, "Don't mess with me!" The cobra hisses loudly. It's a deep, scary sound. Even elephants stop when they see and hear a cobra.

 The cobra's **venom**, or poison, is strong. It can kill an elephant.

The cobra has two long front teeth called **fangs**. They are hollow. Inside is a powerful poison called venom. It can stop an animal's heart. The venom can cause a person to stop breathing. A cobra bite can kill in a few hours.

 Is there a cure for a cobra bite?

Watch out! A cobra bite kills.

Yes. A medicine called **antivenin** saves lives. Zoos that keep cobras usually have it.

Cobras are dangerous, but don't worry. They live far away. Sometimes the cobra's name tells us where they live. The Asian cobra lives in Asia. The Egyptian Cobra lives in Africa. So does the yellow cobra. But you can't tell that from its name.

This yellow cobra lives in Africa. It is also called a cape cobra.

King Cobra

King cobras are the biggest poisonous snakes in the world. They can grow up to 18 feet (5.5 m) long. A king cobra lifts its head and upper body to warn people away. When it does, it stands taller than most grown men! Then it hisses. The hiss sounds like a dog's growl. But king cobras are shy. They do not bother people unless people bother them.

A king cobra lifts its head to warn enemies away.

11

Like the king cobra, Egyptian cobras lays leathery eggs.

 **Q** How many eggs are there?

King cobras are mean, but they care about their eggs. They are the only snakes that build nests for their eggs. The mother snake lays the eggs. Both father and mother stay with the eggs. It takes 45 to 80 days for them to hatch.

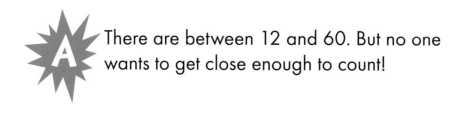There are between 12 and 60. But no one wants to get close enough to count!

Baby cobras take care of themselves. These **hatchlings** can spread their hoods and strike the day they are born. They soon begin to hunt. Like their parents, king cobra hatchlings eat other snakes. They even eat poisonous snakes! They may chew their prey, poking it full of venom.

This baby cobra is small, but it can hunt right away.

A king cobra will stay away
from people if it can.

Cobra Cousins

There are 12 different **species**, or kinds, of cobras. Most have bright bands of color that warn other animals away. Most cobras are 3 to 7 feet (0.9 to 2.1 m) long. Most are thin. They move quickly. Some are more dangerous than others. For example, the Egyptian cobra may go into homes looking for rats. Other cobras are shy and stay away from people.

This cobra found a fish to eat.

 What do they eat?

Most cobras hunt at dawn or dusk. Their good eyesight helps them spot their prey, even when it's dark. They strike out and bite! They may chew a little, but then they swallow the prey whole. Their stomach acids **digest** it. Cobras may not eat again for days or weeks after a big meal.

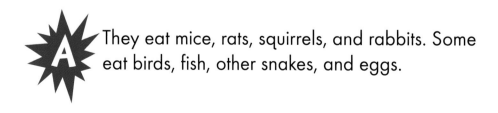
They eat mice, rats, squirrels, and rabbits. Some eat birds, fish, other snakes, and eggs.

Some cobras can spit venom. Spitting cobras have an opening at the tip of each fang. They can spray venom up to 7 feet (2.1 m). Spitting cobras aim for the eyes of their prey. A hit to the eye causes pain and blindness. That's when the cobra moves in for the kill.

A spitting cobra shoots venom from its fangs.

**Snake charmers make
these cobras dance.**

 Q Are cobras deaf?

Cobra Senses

Maybe you've seen pictures of a cobra dancing to a snake charmer's flute. Is the man charming the cobra with his music? That's what he wants people to believe. But it is not true. The cobra cannot hear the music. Instead, it watches the man and follows his movements.

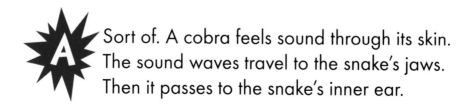 Sort of. A cobra feels sound through its skin. The sound waves travel to the snake's jaws. Then it passes to the snake's inner ear.

This king cobra is
watching for prey.

Cobras have excellent eyesight. They can see prey that is over 300 feet (90 m) away. That's the length of a football field.

But cobras have no sense of taste. They use their tongues to collect smells. A special organ at the top of their mouths tells them when they smell something good to eat.

Enemies?

Few animals dare attack the cobra. Only the mongoose is fast enough to do so. Mongooses are small furry animals that live in Africa and Asia. Sometimes, they dart at the cobra's head and bite the back of its neck. It's a killing blow.

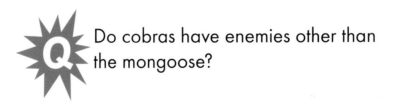 Do cobras have enemies other than the mongoose?

A mongoose is the cobra's only enemy.

 No. The cobra is too quick and dangerous.

There is still much to learn about cobras. Scientists who study snakes say that cobras are hard to find. It is even harder to track them. Some scientists put small radio **transmitters** on some king cobras. The radios sent signals to the scientists. The scientists have learned about how cobras behave. They hope to learn even more.

Cobras are mysterious snakes. Scientists still learn new facts.

Glossary

antivenin Medicine used to treat snake bites.

digest To change food into energy.

fang A long, sharp tooth filled with poison.

hatchling A young bird, reptile, or fish just hatched from an egg.

prey An animal that is hunted for food.

species A kind or group of animals that share certain characteristics.

transmitter Small radios put on animals that send signals to scientists.

venom Poison produced by some animals, like cobras.